Horses in Action!

A POSTER BOOK

Text by **Kathryn Navarra**

Horse Power

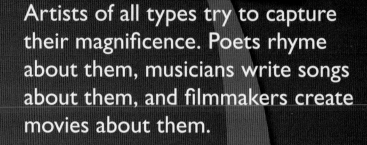

Horses are among the loveliest and most graceful animals on the planet. Whether competing in a horse show, playing in the pasture, or roaming the open range, they move freely and effortlessly.

Artists of all types try to capture their magnificence. Poets rhyme about them, musicians write songs about them, and filmmakers create movies about them.

If you are lucky enough to ride, you know how free you feel as your horse gallops beneath you. Even if you do not ride a horse, you can sense a horse's soothing energy just by looking at pictures of one. In the words of Winston Churchill (prime minister of Great Britain during World War II), "There is something about the outside of a horse that is good for the inside of a man."

In these 30 posters, you will have a chance to see all types of horses in action. As you read the story behind each poster, you will learn a little more about how horses play and live. You will also discover activities you can try, the differences among breeds, and the unspoken words horses use to talk to you.

Taking Flight

This jumper glides over a water obstacle and carefully times his landing so that his hooves do not get wet. Water jumps are popular in show jumping (also known as stadium jumping) contests. These jumps, up to 16 feet across, are the widest in the competition.

Up, Up, and Away

In stadium jumping, a horse and rider must jump a **course** (path) of tall, wide, and colorful obstacles without knocking anything down. Winners are chosen based on speed and accuracy. If a horse will not jump a fence, this is a **refusal.** Any horse with three refusals is eliminated. The riders try to finish in the fastest time with the fewest points. **Faults** (points) are added to the score every time a rail is knocked off during a jump.

Where Did the Sport Come From?

Show jumping, one of the newer equine sports, started in England in 1907. It is now one of the equine events included in the summer Olympic Games. Stadium jumping can be held as a separate event or as part of a Three-Day Event competition in which horse and rider must compete in dressage and cross-country jumping as well.

Fun Fact

Jumps are made to be distracting and test a horse's ability to focus. In the past, some of the fences had giant bright yellow smiley faces on either side. Others featured models of Shamu, the whale from Sea World.

photograph on previous page: © **Shawn Hamilton/CLIX Photography** • *Horses in Action! A Poster Book,* **Storey Publishing**

Power Struggle

These two wild horses are sorting out where they rank in the group. This rank is called the **pecking order.** All horses that live together either in the wild or in the pasture put themselves into different ranks.

Choosing Ranks

Many different things can affect a horse's place in the herd. The horse's size, his age, his strength, and the length of time he has been in the herd decide his standing. Determining one's rank can get rough, as it has with the two horses that are striking out at one another in this picture. Once the new horse learns his place, they'll calm down.

Herding Up

While a **stallion** (an adult male horse) is responsible for protecting the herd from danger, the **alpha mare** (the strongest female horse in a herd) is the leader of the group. She is first in line for food, water, or attention from her human caretakers. Even though the leader is pushy, she and the others form a tight bond. This can be noticeable when one horse leaves the barn. Those left behind may whinny and pace until their buddy returns.

Fun Fact

On hot, sunny days when flies are pesky, one horse will stand beside another, head to tail, so that they can sweep the bugs off each other. Just as people ask friends for help with a hard-to-reach itch, horses will scratch the backs of other horses in the group.

photograph on previous page: © **Thomas Dressler/ardea.com** • *Horses in Action! A Poster Book,* Storey Publishing

Airs Above the Ground

Suspended above the ground, this Lipizzan (or Lipizzaner) is showing off his powerful muscles while performing the **croupade.** This move is similar to the **capriole.** Instead of kicking out his back legs, however, this horse tucks them beneath him.

A School for Horses

The Spanish Riding School in Vienna, Austria, trains Lipizzan horses. The school is the oldest and one of the most famous classical **dressage** (advanced training of a horse) riding academies in the world. Trainers teach advanced dressage and the acrobatic Airs Above the Ground. Riders learn the best ways to communicate with their horses. Only citizens of the European Union can apply to the school. They must be at least 15 years old and have excellent riding skills.

Shall We Dance?

Lipizzans know how to follow the music perfectly, so they look like they are dancing. Like ballerinas, they are elegant and beautiful. It's hard to take your eyes off a Lipizzan when he is performing. For these reasons, their performances are often called the Equestrian Ballet.

Fun Fact

Horses at the Spanish Riding School perform at the Imperial Palace in Vienna. Inside the palace, there is a large riding hall, built in the early 1700s as a place where wealthy children could learn to ride.

photograph on previous page: © **Mark J. Barrett**/www.markjbarrett.com • *Horses in Action! A Poster Book,* **Storey Publishing**

Photo Finish

Racing neck and neck, each of these horses is determined to win and stretch his nose out in front. In close races like this one, a photograph is needed to tell which horse is the winner, even if only by a whisker!

Off to the Races

Thoroughbred flat-track racing tests the speed of horses running on a dirt or grass surface. The distance of each race is based on the age and experience of the horses in the race. Before a race, some horses are given **handicaps** (extra weight carried in their saddle). Even though Thoroughbreds are the most common racehorses, other breeds are known for speed, too. Quarter Horses are good sprinters, and Standardbreds are good harness racers.

Where Did the Sport Come From?

People have raced their steeds for thousands of years, but modern horse racing developed in England during the 1600s and 1700s. Three races — the Kentucky Derby, the Belmont Stakes, and the Preakness Stakes — make up the Triple Crown, the most famous American racing trophy. To win the Triple Crown, a horse must win all three races in the same year. Only 11 horses in the past 125 years have captured the title.

Fun Fact

Seabiscuit, a Thoroughbred, was an unlikely champion in the 1930s. He was an ugly **colt** (a male horse less than 4 years old) with big, knobby knees. His speed and courage made him famous. A movie and book named for him tell the story of his path to stardom.

photograph on previous page: © Mark J. Barrett/www.markjbarrett.com • *Horses in Action! A Poster Book*, Storey Publishing

Snowy Stampede

A **wrangler** (a ranch worker who handles horses) pushes a herd out of a snowstorm and into a field where water and food are easier to find. Horses have built-in insulation that protects them from the cold. They begin to grow a thick woolly coat at the end of summer to help keep them warm. The new hairs are not noticeable at first.

Baby, It's Cold Outside

Horses usually don't need much help from their owners to stay warm in the winter. A thick coat of hair protects them from bad weather and keeps rain and snow from reaching their skin. Also, the horse's body makes a wax called **sebum** that covers his skin, so even if water makes it past the fuzzy hair, it will just run off the skin.

Warming Up!

The best way to tell if a horse is cold is to feel his ears. If his ears are cold, then you should bring him into the barn or blanket him to warm up. Blankets should be chosen carefully. Stable blankets are not waterproof and should be used only when a horse is kept indoors. Turnout rugs are water-resistant and tough, so they can be used outdoors.

Fun Fact

Skijoring, started in Scandinavia, is similar to waterskiing or dog sledding. The horse pulls a person wearing skis around a track. Some tracks are flat and others include several jumps, like those seen on a ski slope. Montana and New Hampshire both have skijoring events each winter.

An Equine Triathlon

This horse is competing in an Eventing Trial. Like a human triathlon, This event is made up of three parts: **dressage** (precise movements of a horse in response to the rider's signals), **cross country** (a timed jumping course out in the open countryside rather than in a ring), and **stadium jumping** (a timed course where riders jump each obstacle). Careful training has prepared this horse and rider for any surprises they may meet along the course.

Where Did the Sport Come From?

Eventing began in Europe as a military competition to test the ability of **cavalry horses** (horses used to fight wars before tanks were invented). Dressage demonstrated a horse's obedience and how well he would perform in parades. The cross-country section challenged courage and bravery, needed for escaping from an enemy or carrying important letters from one fort to the next. Stadium jumping tested the horse's overall fitness and ability to perform after a long day.

Different Names, Same Event

In Britain the first official name given to the sport was Three-Day Eventing because the competition lasted three days. Americans frequently call the event Combined Training, as multiple disciplines are performed.

Fun Fact

Riders of all ages can try Eventing in beginner and novice classes as well as at higher levels. Eventing is one of the equine disciplines in the summer Olympic Games, first included in 1912.

photograph on previous page: © Amber Heintzberger • *Horses in Action! A Poster Book,* Storey Publishing

Recess

●●●●●●●●●●●●●

This **foal** (young horse) is running so quickly that he seems about to fall over. When a foal is born, his legs are almost as long as an adult horse's legs. If you look closely at the photograph, you can see that this foal's hind legs are as high as his mother's shoulder. The word *foal* describes all baby horses. A **colt** is a male foal and a **filly** is a female.

Good Moms

During his first month of life, a foal is playful and curious but stays close to his mother. Like the **mare** (adult female horse) in this picture, the moms stay nearby and keep a watchful eye out for any signs of danger. Young horses spend much of the day sleeping, lying right down in the grass or on stall bedding.

Growing Up

Foals develop much more quickly than children do. In two years, a young horse has grown as much as a human would after eight years. After that their growth slows, but they still grow faster than humans. Even though horses mature quickly, their bones do not stop growing until they are 4 or 5 years old. If young horses begin a training program that is too difficult for them, they can easily become injured.

Fun Fact

Newborn horses are on their feet much earlier than human babies are. When foals are born they learn how to stand within the first hour of life, and they are standing up by the time they are 3 hours old — important for survival in the wild.

photograph on previous page: © Mark J. Barrett/www.markjbarrett.com • *Horses in Action! A Poster Book*, Storey Publishing

Stretching Out

With one ear tipped to the side and the other pointed straight ahead, this horse seems to be paying attention to someone we cannot see in the photo. His owner may be **free longeing** him (a training method in which the horse is exercised in a round pen without a line attached to him) from the middle of the arena to get him ready for a riding session. Or the photographer could be standing there taking the perfect shot. Either way, this horse is relaxed and happy to be enjoying time outside.

Time for a Warm-Up

Before starting any tough workout, horses need a chance to stretch. Like all athletes, they should start training routines slowly to avoid injury and find their focus. Stabled horses especially enjoy a few minutes of play after standing around all day. This makes it easier for them to pay attention during the lesson and reduces the chance of injury.

How Old Is an Old Horse?

A well-cared-for horse, like the one shown in the picture here, will usually live into his mid-20s, and possibly even into his 30s. The oldest horse is more than 50 years old!

Fun Fact

A horse's teeth can reveal his age. Horses are born with temporary teeth that are eventually replaced with permanent ones. The type of teeth and the wear of each tooth provide clues to help figure how old a horse is. Younger horses have larger, deep grooves in their teeth, but as they age, the grooves become shallower.

photograph on previous page: © Sabine Stuewer/TIERFOTO • *Horses in Action! A Poster Book,* Storey Publishing

Who's the Boss?

These two Friesians are fighting to prove their strength. Each horse is using his hooves and teeth as weapons to teach the other horse who's boss. Friesians appear to descend from wild horses in Europe. They were crossed with Andalusians and other breeds.

A Highly Prized Horse

In Holland, having a Friesian stallion accepted for breeding is a very big honor. Every February, the best 3- and 4-year-old stallions are brought to one location in Holland and judged. Judges look for balance and action in the front and hind legs. Those selected are sent to a school to be trained. After training, only one or two horses are selected to be official breeding stallions. These horses are marked with an F on the side of their neck.

What Are They Saying?

Each stallion is giving warning signs to the other. The first stallion's open mouth shows that he is angry. The second horse is biting at the other horse's throat to let his enemy know he is not going to lose.

Fun Fact

Stallion battles are both mental and physical. Usually the weaker horse can sense when he is going to lose and will stop fighting before he gets hurt. Most of the time, ranch or farm horses that "fight" in the pasture are playing more than fighting.

photograph on previous page: © Sabine Stuewer/TIERFOTO • *Horses in Action! A Poster Book*, Storey Publishing

Home on the Range

Run to the right, now to the left! This horse is trying to escape the **lassos** (ropes with a loop at one end) of these cowboys. He may have broken loose from the ranch, or he may be wild. Wild horses, called **Mustangs,** still roam the open land in the western part of the United States.

Where Did Wild Horses Come From?

Spanish explorers brought horses to the New World in the 1500s. "Mustang" comes from the Spanish word *musteño,* which means "stray horse" or "without an owner." Native Americans had never seen horses before the Spanish arrived. There was no word in their language for "horse" so they called them "big dogs." Once Native Americans started to ride, they were able to hunt more easily, fight better, and move from place to place.

Where Are They Today?

There are only about 25,000 Mustangs on open land today. Most of them live in Nevada and Montana. The Bureau of Land Management, the part of the U.S. government in charge of controlling their population, hosts an adoption program to find good homes for some of them.

Fun Fact

Even though many people call the Mustang wild, it is actually a **feral horse.** A feral horse is a horse that now lives in the wild but has ancestors that were trained by humans. The only true wild horse left in the world is Przewalski's Horse, which comes from Asia.

Pull That Load

These **driving horses** (horses used to pull a wagon or cart) are working together to pull the carriage attached behind them. The driver of this pair has asked them to *haw* or turn left. To go right, the driver would have given the command *gee*.

Drive On

This pair of horses is pulling a carriage. The carriage could have two wheels or four, depending on the type of cart and what it is used for. There are two main types of competitive carriage driving. **Classical driving** is performed in an arena. It is judged on how well the horses move and how the driver and the cart look. **Combined driving** is made up of a cross-country course, a driven dressage pattern, and a timed cones course.

What Breed Is It?

Norwegian Fjords are thought to be one of the world's oldest and purest breeds of horse. Over 4,000 years ago, the horses migrated to western Norway. Almost all Fjords are **dun** (tan with black markings). A perfectly straight line of black hairs grows in the middle of the white mane along the horse's neck. The mane is cut to show off that stripe.

Fun Fact

Although any breed of horse can be used as a carriage horse, some are more suited to it than others. It is very important to train the horse so that the cart doesn't scare him.

photograph on previous page: © **Mark J. Barrett/www.markjbarrett.com** • *Horses in Action! A Poster Book,* Storey Publishing

And They're Off!

These horses are in a tough competition called a steeplechase, which includes both running and jumping. The jockey must work hard to keep her balance. She does not want to slow the horse's momentum as he leaps into the air.

Off to the Races

Steeplechases challenge a horse's speed and ability to jump over **fences,** or jumps. The jumps make a steeplechase different from regular racing. The horses race out of the starting gate and approach the fences together, often leaping over them at the same time.

Where Did the Sport Come From?

The sport of steeplechasing started in Ireland in the 1700s when riders would race cross-country from church steeple to church steeple. Today most steeplechases take place on the inside of a Thoroughbred flat track. Unlike stadium jumping, the obstacles used in a steeplechase are made to look natural and include brush hedges and post-and-rail fences.

Fun Fact

The best-known steeplechase event is called the Grand National and is held on the Aintree track in Liverpool, England. The book and movie *National Velvet* describe this race. Each horse must complete two trips around the track, making each race a total of 4½ miles. There are 16 fences, and 14 of them have to be jumped twice. Red Rum was the most successful Grand National Champion racehorse. He won the race in 1973, 1974, and 1976.

Kick Up Your Heels

Romping like kids outside at recess, these young horses are playfully kicking up their heels and enjoying the nice weather. Their eyes, ears, and body position show that they are only having fun and not fighting. Their ears are turned to hear each other but are not pinned back. Their eyes look friendly.

Horse Play

Horses learn how to play with each other as **foals** (young horses). Just like kids, horses tease their friends into play, nipping or nudging their buddies into games. **Fillies** (young female horses) do not play as roughly as **colts** (young male horses less than 4 years old) do, but they still participate in a round of tag. Some may even pick up loose items like sticks with their teeth and fling them from side to side.

What Breed Is It?

These horses playing in the field are Clydesdales. They can grow to between 16.2 and 18 **hands** high. (Hands are a measure of a horse's height. Each hand equals 4 inches.) Typically they weigh 1,700 to 2,000 pounds, but some adult males can weigh up to 2,200 pounds. Clydesdales are **draft horses** (large, heavy horses used for pulling) and are originally from Scotland. Before tractors, they were used to plow fields. Today they are used to pull wagons in shows and parades just for fun.

Fun Fact

Clydesdales can be recognized by their **feathers.** Feathers are the long, white fluffy hairs on their legs. The silky hair highlights their powerful yet graceful movements.

photograph on previous page: © Mark J. Barrett/www.markjbarrett.com • *Horses in Action! A Poster Book,* Storey Publishing

Playing Polo

With the ball just inches from his hooves, the horse slows down just enough to give his rider a chance to hit it down the field during a game of polo. Polo ponies must be quick and responsive to their riders. Not true ponies, they are actually full-sized horses, most commonly Thoroughbreds or sport-breed mixes.

Polo Basics

Two teams of riders, four riders on each, use long wooden mallets to hit the ball down the field and score points. Goals count only if the rider is on his horse. The game has either four or six **chukkers** (7-minute periods). An outdoor polo field is about the same size as 10 football fields! Polo can be played on smaller indoor fields, but then teams have three riders each. Some polo matches are even played in the snow.

Where Did the Sport Come From?

The first polo match in the United States was played in 1876. Polo may be one of the oldest horse sports. Some historians think the people from the country of Persia (now Iran) played polo thousands of years ago. Back when the army used horses on the battlefields, polo matches were used as training exercises for the horses and their riders.

Fun Fact

At the middle and end of a polo match, the people watching are invited to walk onto the polo field and replace the **divots** (holes) in the grass made by the horses' hooves. Fixing the divots is fun for the crowd and repairs the field.

photograph on previous page: © Mark J. Barrett/www.markjbarrett.com • *Horses in Action! A Poster Book*, Storey Publishing

Equine Royalty

This Andalusian Horse is performing an acrobatic move called the **capriole.** In order to leap into the air, he tucks his front legs and kicks out strongly with his hind legs. Horses trained to perform the capriole were often used in battle because the powerful kick could knock over enemies.

Where Did the Breed Come From?

The Andalusian breed is named for the region it comes from: Andalusia, Spain, on the Iberian Peninsula. Ancient Greeks and Romans praised the breed as one of the finest warhorses, because it is strong and athletic and has a very even temper. Most Andalusians are gray or white, although they can also be tan or reddish brown. Very few are black, **dun** (tan with black markings), or Palomino.

A Master of Dressage

During the Renaissance period (A.D. 1400–1600), the Andalusian was called the royal horse of Europe and was the breed of choice to perform in royal courts. Riding academies throughout Europe used the Andalusian in high-level training. Because of their ability to perform so elegantly, Andalusians were used to develop other breeds like the world-famous Lipizzan stallions (see poster "Airs Above the Ground").

Fun Fact

When some groups of Lipizzan stallions tour, several Andalusians are part of the cast. They perform movements like the capriole, seen here, as well as exercises with riders, to illustrate the Lipizzan's heritage.

photograph on previous page: © Bob Langrish • *Horses in Action! A Poster Book,* Storey Publishing

Pretty Pinto

Pricked-up ears and a raised tail indicate that this horse has spotted something off in the distance. Known for a flashy coat, the Pinto, like the one seen here, has become popular because of its colorful markings.

A Colorful Horse

The Pinto is a color breed that is described based on the color of its coat rather than its family history or **conformation** (build). A Pinto's coloring is called **tobiano** or **overo.** A tobiano looks like a white horse with large patches of brown or black. An overo horse appears to be a colored horse with white patches of hair that start on his belly and reach toward his neck, tail, back, and legs. An overo has a dark mane and tail and usually has a **bald face** (white covering the face).

A Pinto for Every Rider

The Pinto can be divided into four types: the Stock, Hunter, Saddle, and Pleasure. The Stock type has the conformation of a Quarter Horse and is used in Western events. Hunter-type Pintos usually have Thoroughbred breeding and are hunter-jumper horses. Saddlebreds, Hackneys, and Tennessee Walking Horses are the Saddle type, and Arabians, Morgans, and Welsh Ponies are the Pleasure type.

Fun Fact

Even though the Pinto is most commonly thought of as belonging to Native American tribes, the breed was actually brought here from Spain. The Arabian Horse may have influenced the development of the Pinto. However, a full-blooded registered Arabian cannot have pinto coloring.

photograph on previous page: © Sabine Stuewer/TIERFOTO • *Horses in Action! A Poster Book,* Storey Publishing

Horseback Gymnastics!

This horse's back has become a stage for gymnastics! It's hard to believe, but this horse is steadily **cantering** (a 3-beat gait faster than a trot) while his rider performs daring stunts.

Hanging Around

The woman in this picture is using a trick-riding saddle, a Western saddle that has handles attached to the front and back to help the rider perform tricks. Most routines are performed at a gallop, so they are very difficult and dangerous. Vaulting is similar to trick riding but uses a **surcingle** (a belt around the horse's belly). Both trick riders and vaulters do handstands or shoulder stands, often performing to music.

Where Did the Sport Come From?

Ancient stone paintings show people standing on the backs of horses. The Roman Games, held 2,000 years ago, included events where people performed dance movements set to music on a horse's back. During the Middle Ages (A.D. 500–1500), knights trained for battle by doing gymnastics routines on the backs of their horses. Today, equestrian vaulting is one of seven **equine** (horse) events in the Olympic Games. When the sport was first introduced at the Olympics in 1920, it was called Artistic Riding.

Fun Fact

Vaulting is a team and individual sport for children and adults. There are three types: recreational vaulting, taught by local clubs just for fun; competitive vaulting, for trained athletes; and therapeutic vaulting, for people with mental or physical disabilities.

photograph on previous page: © Lara Dziurdzy/Briarwood Photography • *Horses in Action! A Poster Book*, Storey Publishing

Jump into Action

With his knees tucked and hind legs stretched out, this horse sails over a **spread** (wide jump) without touching any of the poles. A rider must carefully plan and guide her horse to each fence. An experienced rider knows how far her horse's legs reach during the **canter** (a 3-beat gait faster than a trot). For most horses, one canter stride equals 12 to 14 human paces.

Double Fences

The jump in this picture is an **oxer.** An oxer consists of two fences set up one in front of the other so that a horse must soar over both at the same time. Each course is made up of four or five basic obstacles.

Jump Over This!

The **vertical jump** is similar to the jump in the photo but with one fence instead of two. Even though it seems easy, it is one of the most difficult obstacles for a horse to jump. The **wall jump** is built to look like a solid brick wall, but it is actually a row of loose pieces that will tumble to the ground if hit by the horse's legs. A **combination jump** has two fences like the oxer, but there is space in between for the horse to land.

Fun Fact

Every course is different, so it is important to walk it ahead of time. This is the rider's chance to look at each jump up close.

photograph on previous page: © **Bob Langrish** • *Horses in Action! A Poster Book*, **Storey Publishing**

Playing Rough

It looks as if this dark brown horse could be saying, "I told you to knock it off!" to the tan or dun horse. Threatening to punish the other horse, he shows his teeth and strikes out with his legs.

Back Off!

Using his hooves and teeth, the darker horse is letting the lighter-colored horse know he misbehaved by coming into his space. Luckily, humans do not need to be harsh to let a horse know he has misbehaved. Usually a firm voice is enough discipline to teach the horse a lesson.

Do You See What I See?

Sometimes one horse may punish another for sneaking up on him or hiding in his **blind spot** (the area in which a horse cannot see anything). Horses have the largest eyes of any land mammal, but it is important to remember that if you do not see a horse's eyes, he cannot see you. A rider sitting in a saddle on the horse's back is in a blind spot, and a person standing right behind a horse's tail cannot be seen either. A horse will also never be able to see objects directly in front of him where his forehead is. He can, however, see objects at the tip of his nose.

Fun Fact

Horses can see almost as well as humans. In the past, it was thought they could not see far away, but recent studies have proved that they can see distant objects.

photograph on previous page: © age fotostock/Superstock • *Horses in Action! A Poster Book*, Storey Publishing

Eight Long Seconds

This horse will try to do many things to make this cowboy fall in the dirt. He may try leaping, spinning, dropping his head, or gritting his teeth and **bucking** (leaping off the ground and kicking out with his back legs). The cowboy has to hang on very tight to the rope around the horse's belly to keep from falling off.

Getting Ready for Action

Before the rodeo starts, the horse is kept in a **chute** (a tight space between metal gates) so that he can't move around. While he is in this chute, the rider drops onto his back. The rider wraps a rope that is attached to the horse around his hand. This is his only way to hold on. The rider signals for the gate to open and horse and rider burst out together. The rider must stay on for 8 seconds or he receives no score.

Different Styles

There are two kinds of bronc riding: bareback and saddle. Cowboys who are bareback riders hold on to a strap that is wrapped around the horse's belly. The cowboy in this picture is a bareback rider. Cowboys who are saddle bronc riders grip a lead rope that is attached to one side of the halter. Some cowboys think saddle bronc riding is the toughest rodeo event to master because they must learn so many technical skills in order to win.

Fun Fact

Bronc riding began in the days of the Old West. The contest showed which cowboys could ride the wildest, most untrained horses.

photograph on previous page: © **Bob Langrish** • *Horses in Action! A Poster Book*, Storey Publishing

Sir Lancelot

Dressed as a knight, this rider is galloping toward his opponent to begin a **joust** (a game where one rider tries to knock another rider off his horse). He will use his **lance** (a 10-foot-long wooden pole) to try to unseat his opponent.

Surely You Joust

In olden times, knights started the joust with three weapons: the lance, a one-handed sword, and a **rondel** (a smaller weapon more like a dagger). The first knight to fall off his horse lost the match. If both knights fell off at the same time, they would fight with their swords. If a knight lost his sword, he would use his last weapon, the rondel.

Where Did the Sport Come From?

Jousting was popular from the 1300s to the 1500s. Winning a joust greatly increased a knight's honor and wealth. Knights learned to joust on a wooden horse with wheels. Several men were needed to pull the wooden horse toward the target. When the knight had improved his skills, he moved to a real horse. After the 1400s, knights started wearing a full suit of armor, and horses wore protective gear, too. A **chanfron** (a metal plate worn on the horse's head) shielded the horse's face from an oncoming lance.

Fun Fact

Jousting is the state sport of Maryland. Tournaments are held to determine the best jouster in the area. Instead of charging at other knights, competitors race toward a line of rings hanging in the air. The knight who spears the most rings with his lance wins. Even 4-H clubs participate!

photograph on previous page: © Keith Woosey • *Horses in Action! A Poster Book*, Storey Publishing

Racing on White Turf

Light, fluffy snow flies into the faces of jockeys and fans alike as Thoroughbreds race through the snow toward the finish line. Racing in the snow began in 1907 on the frozen lake at St. Moritz, in the Swiss Alps.

And They're Off

This traditional horse race on the ice is called White Turf and is held the first three Sundays of February in St. Moritz. In 2007 the event is 100 years old. Nearly 25,000 people come to watch the annual event. It is said that the race has the highest **purse** (amount of money paid to the winners) of any horse race in the world.

Where Did the Breed Come From?

Thoroughbreds are famous for their speed and their racing abilities. They also compete in Eventing and Hunter/Jumper Trials. All Thoroughbreds can be traced back to three **foundation horses** (horses that were the start of the breed): the Darley Arabian, the Godolphin Arabian (also called the Godolphin Turk), and the Byerly Turk. The first name is the horse's owner and the second name identifies from which country the horse came. Samuel Gist brought the first Thoroughbred to the American colonies in 1730.

Fun Fact

All Thoroughbred horses that live in the northern hemisphere (north of the equator) are given the standard birthday of January 1. Even though a horse born on May 25 or July 31 will only be 6 months old the following January, he is officially considered 1 year old.

Glossary

Alpha mare The strongest female horse in a herd.

Breed A kind of horse.

Bronc An untamed horse.

Canter A 3-beat gait faster than a trot.

Color breed A type of horse identified by the color of its coat.

Colt A male horse younger than 4 years.

Conformation Build.

Cremello A very light tan, almost white.

Draft horse Large heavy horse used for pulling.

Dressage Precise movements of a horse in response to the rider's signals.

Driving horse A horse used to pull a wagon or cart.

Dun Tan with black markings.

Equine Horse.

Farrier A person who puts horseshoes on a horse's feet.

Feathers Long, white, fluffy hairs on a horse's legs.

Feral horse A horse that now lives in the wild but has ancestors that were trained by humans.

Filly A young female horse.

Foal A baby horse.

Foundation horses Horses that were the start of a breed.

Free longeing A training method in which the horse is exercised in a round pen without a line attached to his halter.

Hands A measure of a horse's height. A hand equals 4 inches.

Herd A family group of wild horses.

Mare An adult female horse.

Mustang A wild horse.

Paint A horse with Pinto coloring and with a Quarter Horse or Paint Horse as his parent.

Piebald A horse with black and white Pinto markings.

Pinto A horse with large patches of color.

Skewbald A horse with Pinto markings in colors other than black and white.

Stallion An adult male horse.

Veterinarian A doctor who works with animals.

Wrangler A ranch worker who handles horses.

Edited by Deborah Burns and Sarah Guare

Art direction by Vicky Vaughn

Cover and text design and production by Kristy L. MacWilliams

Cover photograph © MillersReflections

Additional interior photographs © Mark J. Barrett/www.markjbarrett.com, title page and intro page; © Sabine Stuewer/TIERFOTO, glossary page; © age fotostock/Superstock, this page

The information in this book is true and complete to the best of our knowledge. All recommendations are made without guarantee on the part of the author or Storey Publishing. The author and publisher disclaim any liability in connection with the use of this information. For additional information, please contact Storey Publishing, 210 MASS MoCA Way, North Adams, MA 01247.

Storey books are available for special premium and promotional uses and for customized editions. For further information, please call 1-800-793-9396.

Printed in Hong Kong by Elegance

10 9 8 7 6 5 4 3 2 1